ISOLDE

ISOLDE. FROM "THE STUDIO"

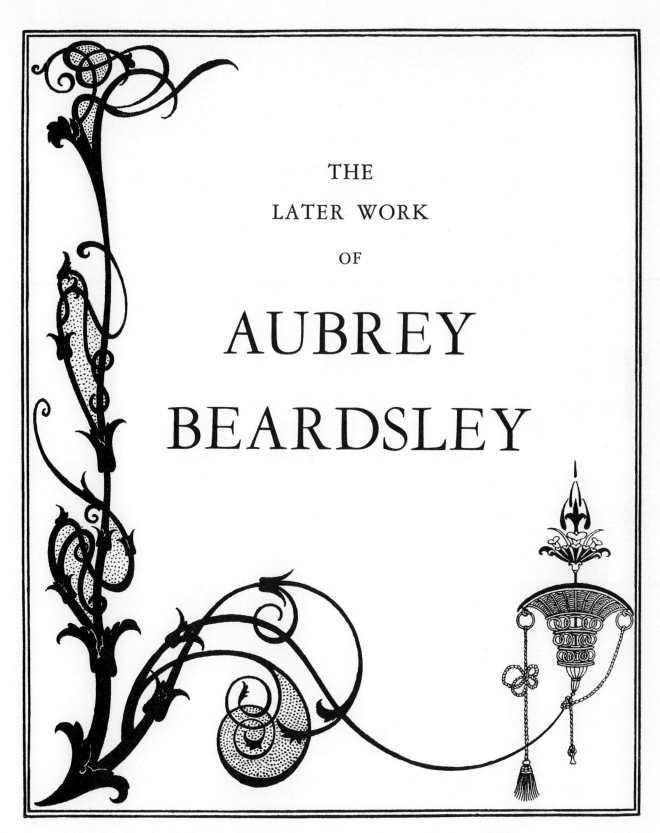

THE

LATER WORK

OF

AUBREY

BEARDSLEY

DOVER PUBLICATIONS, INC., NEW YORK

This Dover edition, first published in 1967, is an unabridged republication of the revised 1930 edition of the work originally published by John Lane, The Bodley Head. The present edition differs in the following respects:

Two of the four plates printed in color in earlier editions (there was no color in the 1930) are reproduced here in color, in addition to their black-and-white reproductions in the 1930 numerical sequence. The other two plates, Nos. 75 and 76 of the present volume, were originally printed in green ink.

The frontispiece and title-page frame of the original editions now appear in their proper numerical sequence as Plates 1 and 2.

The reproductions in this volume have been made from the best available editions or collections of Beardsley's work.

International Standard Book Number: 0-486-21817-1
Library of Congress Catalog Card Number: 67-21706

MANUFACTURED IN THE UNITED STATES OF AMERICA

DOVER PUBLICATIONS, INC.
180 VARICK STREET
NEW YORK, N.Y. 10014

LIST OF PLATES

LIST OF PLATES

* Also in color between Plates 20 and 21.   † Also in color as the frontispiece.

LIST OF PLATES

LIST OF PLATES

LIST OF PLATES

PUBLISHER'S NOTE

MY warmest thanks are due to Mr. Frederick H. Evans for his assistance in tracing several drawings, the existence of which was unknown to me; also to the possessors of originals, whose name I give beneath each plate, by whose courtesy I have been enabled to reproduce many hitherto unpublished specimens of Beardsley's work.

There has been considerable rearrangement of the plates. Many that originally appeared in the "Early Work" are now transferred to this volume, and conversely, in order to preserve a proper chronological sequence.

PLATES

From a private portrait study by Frederick H. Evans.

Plate I

Plate 2

Plate 3

DESIGN FOR FRONTISPIECE OF
"PLAYS," BY JOHN DAVIDSON

Plate 4

DESIGN FOR TITLE-PAGE OF
"PLAYS," BY JOHN DAVIDSON

Plate 5

DESIGN FOR COVER OF "THE
YELLOW BOOK" PROSPECTUS

MFA PHOTOGRAPHY
HAND BOOK
1986-7

Plate 6

COVER DESIGN FOR "THE
YELLOW BOOK," VOLUME I

DESIGN FOR REVERSE COVER
OF "THE YELLOW BOOK"

Plate 8

TITLE-PAGE ORNAMENT FOR "THE
YELLOW BOOK," VOLUME I ❦ ❦

Plate 9

L'ÉDUCATION SENTIMENTALE.
FROM "THE YELLOW BOOK,"
VOLUME I

Plate 10

NIGHT PIECE. FROM "THE
YELLOW BOOK," VOLUME I

Plate 11

PORTRAIT OF MRS. PATRICK CAMPBELL.
FROM "THE YELLOW BOOK," VOLUME I

Plate 12

BOOK-PLATE. FROM "THE
YELLOW BOOK," VOLUME I

Plate 13

COVER DESIGN FOR "THE YELLOW BOOK," VOLUME II

Plate 14

TITLE-PAGE ORNAMENT FOR "THE YELLOW BOOK," VOLUME II ❧ ❧

Plate 15

COMEDY-BALLET OF MARIONETTES, I
FROM "THE YELLOW BOOK," VOLUME II

Plate 16

COMEDY-BALLET OF MARIONETTES, II
FROM "THE YELLOW BOOK," VOLUME II

Plate 17

COMEDY-BALLET OF MARIONETTES, III
FROM " THE YELLOW BOOK," VOLUME II

Plate 18

GARÇONS DE CAFÉ. FROM "THE
YELLOW BOOK," VOLUME II ❧

Plate 19

THE SLIPPERS OF CINDERELLA. FROM
"THE YELLOW BOOK," VOLUME II

Plate 20

PORTRAIT OF MADAME RÉJANE. FROM
"THE YELLOW BOOK," VOLUME II

MADAME RÉJANE

Plate 21

COVER DESIGN FOR "THE YELLOW
BOOK," VOLUME III ❧ ❧ ❧

Plate 22

TITLE-PAGE DESIGN. FROM " THE
YELLOW BOOK," VOLUME III

ANDREAS. MANTEGNA.
PAINTER.
AND.
ENGRAVER. OF PADVA.
1L91 — 1506.

PORTRAIT OF MANTEGNA (BY PHILIP
BROUGHTON). FROM "THE YELLOW
BOOK," VOLUME III

Plate 23

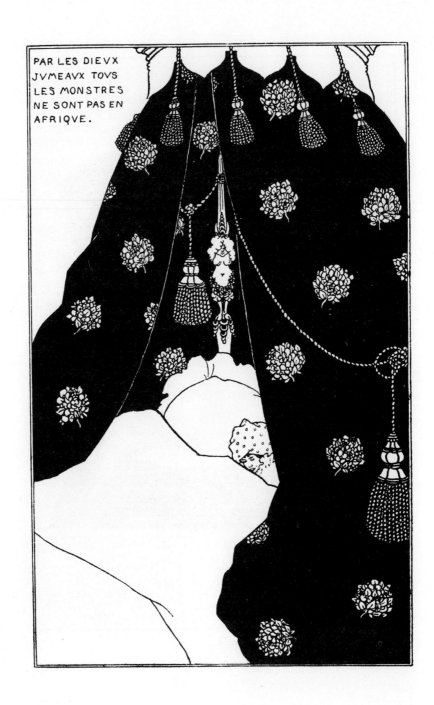

Plate 24

PORTRAIT OF HIMSELF. FROM "THE YELLOW BOOK," VOLUME III 🐂 🐂

Plate 25

LADY GOLD'S ESCORT. FROM "THE
YELLOW BOOK," VOLUME III ❧ ❧

Plate 26

THE WAGNERITES. FROM "THE
YELLOW BOOK," VOLUME III

Plate 27

LA DAME AUX CAMÉLIAS. FROM
"THE YELLOW BOOK," VOLUME III

Plate 28

"FROM A PASTEL" (BY ALBERT FOSCHTER). FROM "THE YELLOW BOOK," VOLUME III

Plate 29

COVER DESIGN FOR "THE
YELLOW BOOK," VOLUME IV

Plate 30

DESIGN FOR TITLE-PAGE. FROM
" THE YELLOW BOOK," VOLUME IV

THE MYSTERIOUS ROSE GARDEN.
FROM "THE YELLOW BOOK,"
VOLUME IV

Plate 31

THE REPENTANCE
OF M^{RS} ....

Plate 32

THE REPENTANCE OF MRS. . . .
FROM "THE YELLOW BOOK,"
VOLUME IV

Plate 33

PORTRAIT OF MISS WINIFRED
EMERY. FROM "THE YELLOW
BOOK," VOLUME IV ❧ ❧

FRONTISPIECE FOR "JUVENAL" FROM
"THE YELLOW BOOK," VOLUME IV

Plate 34

Plate 35

FROM THE FRONTISPIECE FOR
THE SIXTH SATIRE OF JUVENAL
(UNPUBLISHED)

Plate 36

DESIGN FOR "YELLOW BOOK"
COVER (NOT USED)

Plate 37

A POSTER FOR "THE YELLOW BOOK"

Plate 38

MADAME RÉJANE

Plate 39

Plate 40

Plate 41

A POSTER

Plate 42

A POSTER DESIGN. FIRST REPRODUCED
IN "THE POSTER," OCTOBER" 1898

VENUS.

FRONTISPIECE. FOR "VENUS
AND TANNHÄUSER"

Plate 43

THE STORY OF VENUS
AND TANNHÄUSER, IN
WHICH IS SET FORTH AN
EXACT ACCOUNT OF THE
MANNER OF STATE HELD
BY MADAM VENUS, GOD-
DESS AND MERETRIX,
UNDER THE FAMOUS
HÖRSELBERG, AND CON-
TAINING THE ADVEN-
TURES OF TANNHÄUSER
IN THAT PLACE, HIS RE-
PENTANCE, HIS JOURNEY-
ING TO ROME, AND RE-
TURN TO THE LOVING
MOUNTAIN. BY AUBREY
BEARDSLEY.

FRONTISPIECE AND TITLE-PAGE FOR
"VENUS AND TANNHÄUSER"

Plate 44

THE RETURN OF TANNHÄUSER TO
VENUSBERG. REPRODUCED BY
PERMISSION OF MR. J. M. DENT

Plate 45

Plate 46

DESIGN FOR TITLE-PAGE
("VENUS")

Plate 47

DESIGN FOR COVER OF "THE CAM-
BRIDGE A.B.C." BY PERMISSION OF
THE REV. W. AUSTEN LEIGH

DESIGN FOR A GOLF CARD
BY PERMISSION OF MR. R. HIPPESLEY COX

Plate 48

Plate 49

A POSTER DESIGN. BY PERMISSION
OF MR. WILLIAM HEINEMANN

Plate 50

AUTUMN. FROM A DESIGN FOR A
CALENDAR. BY PERMISSION OF
MR. WILLIAM HEINEMANN ❧ ❧

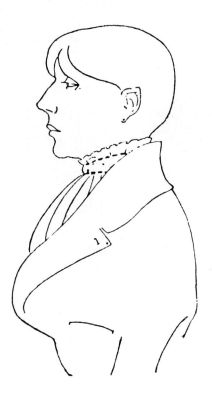

Plate 51

OUTLINE PORTRAIT OF HIMSELF.
FROM "POSTERS IN MINIATURE"

A CHILD AT ITS MOTHER'S BED.
FROM "THE SKETCH." BY PER-
MISSION OF MR. MAX BEERBOHM

Plate 52

THE SCARLET
PASTORALE

Plate 53

THE SCARLET PASTORALE

Plate 54

DESIGN FOR AN INVITATION
CARD ೮ ೮ ೮

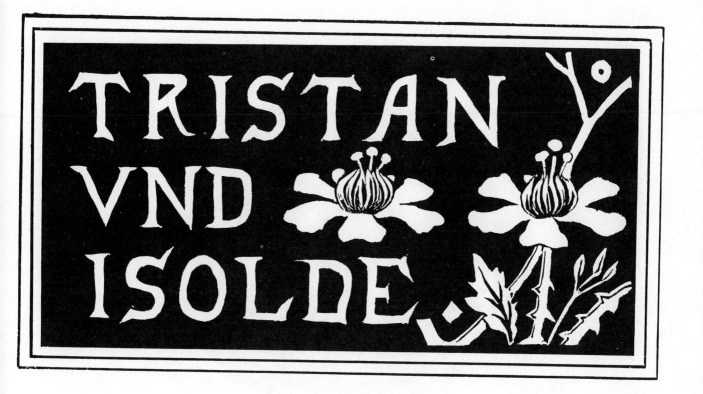

Plate 55

DESIGN FROM THE COVER OF AUBREY
BEARDSLEY'S COPY OF "TRISTAN
UND ISOLDE." BY PERMISSION OF
MR. F. H. EVANS

Plate 56

DESIGN FROM THE COVER OF
AUBREY BEARDSLEY'S COPY OF
"TRISTAN UND ISOLDE." BY
PERMISSION OF MR. F. H. EVANS

ISOLDE

ISOLDE.   FROM "THE STUDIO."
BY PERMISSION OF MR. CHARLES
HOLME   ❦   ❦   ❦   ❦
This plate also appears in color as the fron-
tispiece.

Plate 57

Plate 58

DESIGN FOR A BOOK
COVER

Plate 59

A CATALOGUE COVER

Chopin. Ballade III. Op 47.

CHOPIN, BALLADE III. OP. 47. FROM
"THE STUDIO." BY PERMISSION OF
MR. CHARLES HOLME

Plate 60

Plate 61   A NOCTURNE OF "CHOPIN"

Plate 62

DESIGN FOR FRONTISPIECE OF "EARL
LAVENDER." BY PERMISSION OF
MESSRS. WARD AND DOWNEY ❧ ❧

Plate 63

MESSALINA

Plate 64

TITLE-PAGE ORNAMENT

Plate 65　　　　　　　　　　　PORTRAIT OF MISS LETTY LIND

Plate 66

ATALANTA

Plate 67

COVER DESIGN (SIDE). FROM
BALZAC'S "LA COMÉDIE
HUMAINE" ೪ ೪ ೪

Plate 68

Plate 69

DESIGN FOR FRONTISPIECE TO "AN EVIL MOTHERHOOD." BY PERMISSION OF MR. ELKIN MATHEWS

Plate 70

BLACK COFFEE

Plate 71

DESIGN. FROM THE TITLE-PAGE
OF "THE PARADE"

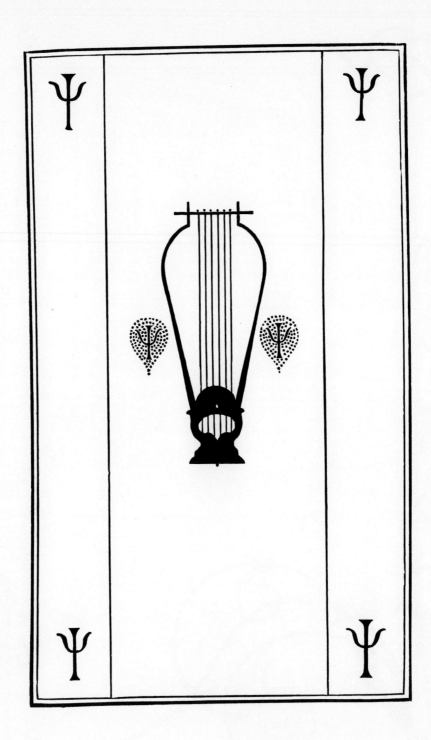

Plate 72

DESIGN FOR COVER OF
WHARTON'S "SAPPHO"

Plate 73

DESIGN FOR FRONT COVER
OF "PIERROT" ❧ ❧

Plate 74

DESIGN FOR TITLE-PAGE
OF "PIERROT"

AVBREY BEARDSLEY.

DESIGN FOR END-PAPER OF "PIERROT"

Plate 75

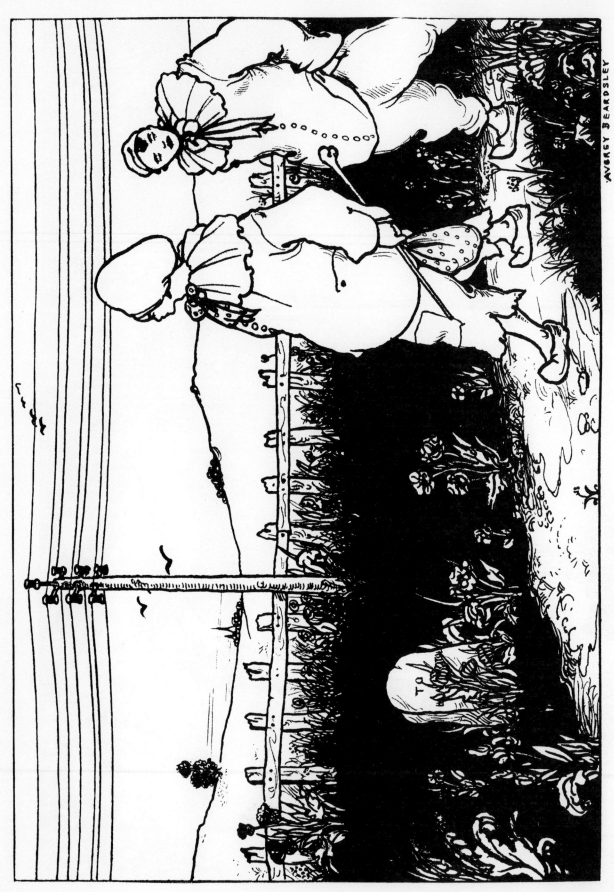

DESIGN FOR END-PAPER OF "PIERROT"

Plate 76

Plate 77

DESIGN FOR REVERSE COVER
OF "PIERROT"

LYSISTRATA.

Plate 78

LYSISTRATA
THIS AND THE FOLLOWING SEVEN DESIGNS
APPEARED IN A PRIVATELY PRINTED EDITION
OF THE "LYSISTRATA" OF ARISTOPHANES

Plate 79   LAMPITO

AUBREY BEARDSLEY.

Plate 80

LYSISTRATA HARANGUING THE
ATHENIAN WOMEN

Plate 81   A DESIGN

Plate 82   AN ATHENIAN WOMAN

Plate 83

MYRRHINA

AVBREY BEARDSLEY

Plate 84   THE HERALD

Plate 85

A DESIGN

THE DREAM

THIS AND THE FOLLOWING EIGHT DESIGNS
ARE REPRODUCED FROM "THE RAPE OF THE
LOCK," PUBLISHED BY JOHN LANE

Plate 86

Plate 87

THE BILLET-DOUX

Plate 88   THE TOILET

Plate 89

THE BARON'S PRAYER

Plate 90   THE BARGE

Plate 91

THE RAPE OF THE LOCK

Plate 92

THE CAVE OF SPLEEN

Plate 93

THE BATTLE OF THE BEAUX
AND THE BELLES

AB.

Plate 94

THE NEW STAR

Plate 95

COVER DESIGN (REDUCED). FROM
THE ORIGINAL EDITION OF "THE
RAPE OF THE LOCK"

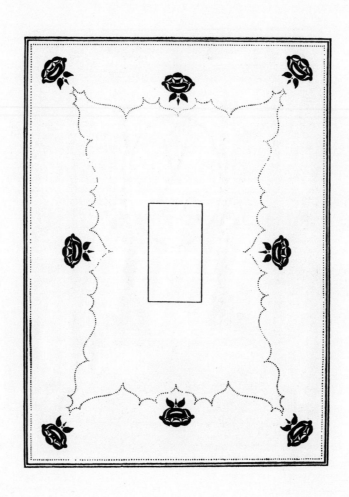

Plate 96

COVER DESIGN. FROM THE BIJOU
EDITION OF "THE RAPE OF THE
LOCK," PUBLISHED BY JOHN LANE

Plate 97   A CATALOGUE COVER

PROSPECTUS
∴∴∴
NUMBER
I
DEC 1ˢᵗ 1895

AVBREY BEARDSLEY

Plate 98

DESIGN FOR THE PROSPECTUS
OF "THE SAVOY"

PROSPECTUS

NUMBER
I

DECEMBER~
1895

AUBREY BEARDSLEY.

ANOTHER DESIGN FOR THE PROSPECTUS
OF "THE SAVOY"

Plate 99

Plate 100

INITIAL. FROM THE PROSPECTUS
OF "THE SAVOY"

Plate 101

SIEGFRIED

THE SAVOY

AUBREY BEARDSLEY. 1896.

Plate 102

COVER DESIGN. FROM "THE SAVOY,"
NO. 1, PUBLISHED BY JOHN LANE

THE SAVOY

AUBREY
BEARDSLEY.
1896.

TITLE-PAGE. FROM "THE SAVOY,"
NOS. 1 AND 2

Plate 103

Plate 104

CONTENTS PAGE. FROM
"THE SAVOY," NO. 1

Plate 105

THE THREE MUSICIANS. FROM
"THE SAVOY," NO. 1

Plate 106

THE THREE MUSICIANS. ANOTHER
DESIGN, WHICH WAS NOT USED IN
"THE SAVOY"

Plate 107

TAILPIECE TO "THE THREE MUSICIANS" 🎵 🎵 🎵 THIS AND THE FOLLOWING THIRTY-THREE DESIGNS ARE REPRODUCED FROM "THE SAVOY," PUBLISHED BY JOHN LANE 🎵

Plate 108

ON DIEPPE BEACH
(THE BATHERS)

MOSKA

Plate 109

THE MOSKA

THE ABBÉ
THIS AND THE FOUR DESIGNS WHICH FOLLOW
APPEARED IN "THE SAVOY," NO. 1, AS ILLUS-
TRATIONS TO "UNDER THE HILL," A ROMANTIC
NOVEL, BY AUBREY BEARDSLEY

Plate 110

Plate 111

THE TOILET OF HELEN

Plate 112

THE FRUIT-BEARERS

Plate 113   A CHRISTMAS CARD

Plate 114

COVER DESIGN. FROM "THE SAVOY," NO. 2

Plate 115

A FOOTNOTE

Plate 116

SAINT ROSE OF LIMA

Plate 117

THE THIRD TABLEAU OF
"DAS RHEINGOLD"

Plate 118

COVER DESIGN. FROM "THE SAVOY," NO. 3

THE
SAVOY

PUCK. FROM "THE SAVOY,"
PUBLISHED BY JOHN LANE

Plate 119

AUBREY BEARDSLEY.

THE COIFFING ℰ ℰ ℰ
THIS AND THE FOLLOWING DESIGN APPEARED
IN "THE SAVOY," NO. 3, ILLUSTRATING "THE
BALLAD OF A BARBER," BY AUBREY BEARDSLEY

Plate 120

Plate 121

CUL-DE-LAMPE

AUBREY BEARDSLEY.

Plate 122   COVER DESIGN. FROM "THE SAVOY," NO. 4

GIULIO FLORIANI.

Plate 123   COVER DESIGN. FROM "THE SAVOY," NO. 5

Plate 124   THE WOMAN IN WHITE

Plate 125

THE FOURTH TABLEAU OF
"DAS RHEINGOLD"

THE DEATH OF PIERROT
"AS THE DAWN BROKE, PIERROT FELL INTO HIS LAST
SLEEP. THEN UPON TIPTOE, SILENTLY UP THE STAIR,
NOISELESSLY INTO THE ROOM, CAME THE COMEDIANS,
ARLECCHINO, PANTALEONE, IL DOTTORE, AND COLUM-
BINA, WHO WITH MUCH LOVE CARRIED AWAY UPON
THEIR SHOULDERS THE WHITE-FROCKED CLOWN OF
BERGAMO; WHITHER, WE KNOW NOT"

Plate 126

Plate 127   COVER DESIGN. FROM "THE SAVOY," NO. 7

AVE ATQVE VALE

AVBREY BEARDSLEY.
AB.

Plate 128

AVE ATQUE VALE: CATULLUS,
CARMEN CI ❦ ❦ ❦

Plate 129

TRISTAN UND ISOLDE

Plate 130   COVER DESIGN. FROM "THE SAVOY," NO. 8

Plate 131

A RÉPÉTITION OF "TRISTAN
UND ISOLDE"

Plate 132

DON JUAN, SGANARELLE,
AND THE BEGGAR. FROM
MOLIÈRE'S "DON JUAN"

MRS PINCHWIFE

Plate 133

MRS. PINCHWIFE

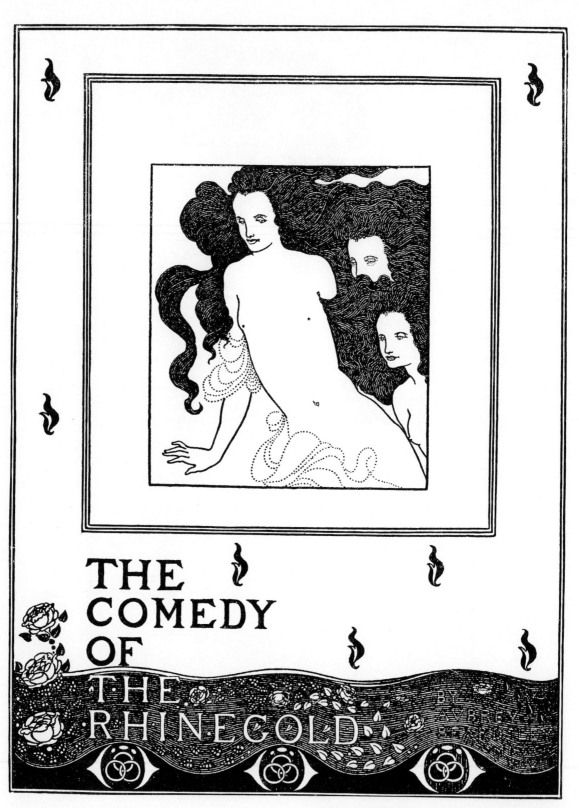

THE
COMEDY
OF
THE
RHINEGOLD

Plate 134

FRONTISPIECE TO THE COMEDY
OF "DAS RHEINGOLD"

Plate 135

FLOSSHILDE.   TO ILLUSTRATE
"DAS   RHEINGOLD" ❧   ❧

Plate 136

ERDA. TO ILLUSTRATE
"DAS RHEINGOLD"

ALBERICH

Plate 137

ALBERICH. TO ILLUSTRATE
"DAS RHEINGOLD"

Plate 138

FELIX MENDELSSOHN
BARTHOLDY

Plate 139

CARL MARIA VON WEBER

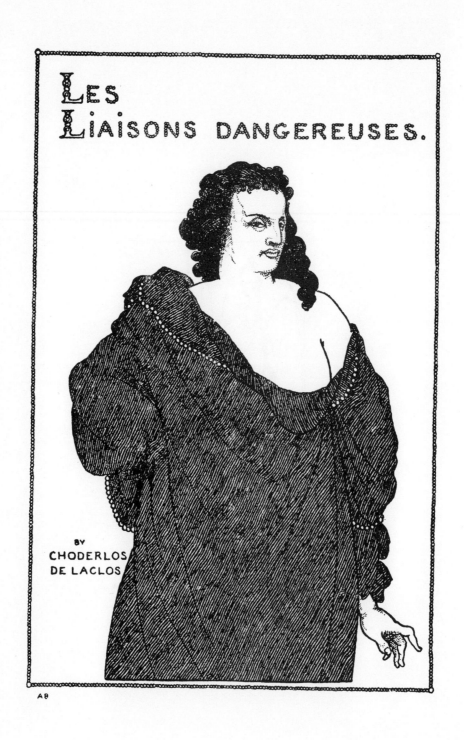

LES LIAISONS DANGEREUSES.

BY
CHODERLOS
DE LACLOS

Plate 140

COUNT VALMONT. FROM "LES
LIAISONS DANGEREUSES"

Plate 141

ET IN ARCADIA EGO

PENCIL SKETCH OF A CHILD. BY
PERMISSION OF MR. FREDERICK
H. EVANS   ❧   ❧   ❧   ❧

Plate 142

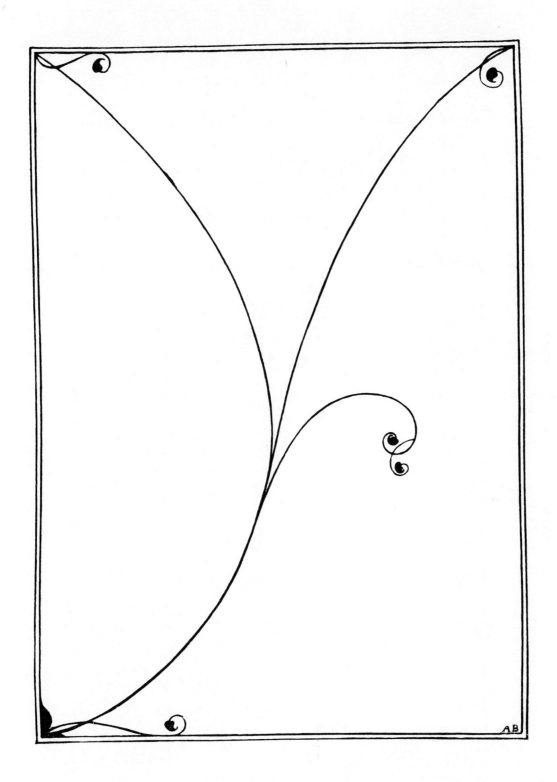

Plate 143

COVER DESIGN. FROM "VERSES,"
BY ERNEST DOWSON

Plate 144

FRONTISPIECE
THIS AND THE FOLLOWING THREE DESIGNS
APPEAR IN THE POEMS OF ERNEST DOWSON,
PUBLISHED BY JOHN LANE

Plate 145

HEADPIECE

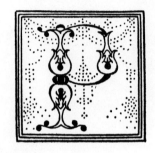

Plate 146

INITIAL

Plate 147

CUL-DE-LAMPE

THE
PIERROT
OF
THE
MINVTE.

Plate 148

COVER DESIGN. FROM "THE
PIERROT OF THE MINUTE,"
PUBLISHED BY JOHN LANE

Plate 149

COVER DESIGN. FROM "THE
SOUVENIRS OF LEONARD" ℰ

BOUTEZ EN AVANT •

Plate 150

COVER DESIGN. FROM "THE
LIFE AND TIMES OF MADAME
DU BARRY"   ℰ   ℰ   ℰ

Plate 151

FRONTISPIECE. FROM "A
BOOK OF BARGAINS"

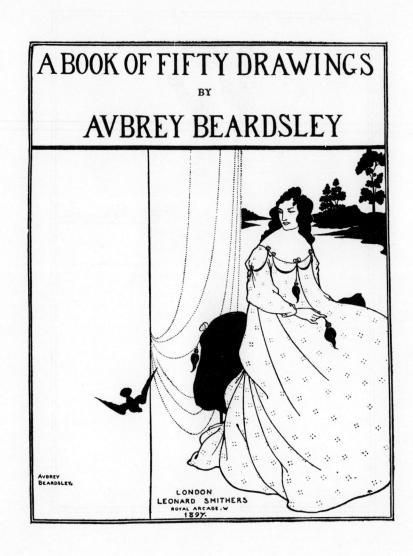

Plate 152

COVER DESIGN. FROM "A
BOOK OF FIFTY DRAWINGS"

Plate 153

SILHOUETTE OF AUBREY
BEARDSLEY ❧ ❧

Plate 154

AUBREY BEARDSLEY'S
BOOK-PLATE ❦ ❦

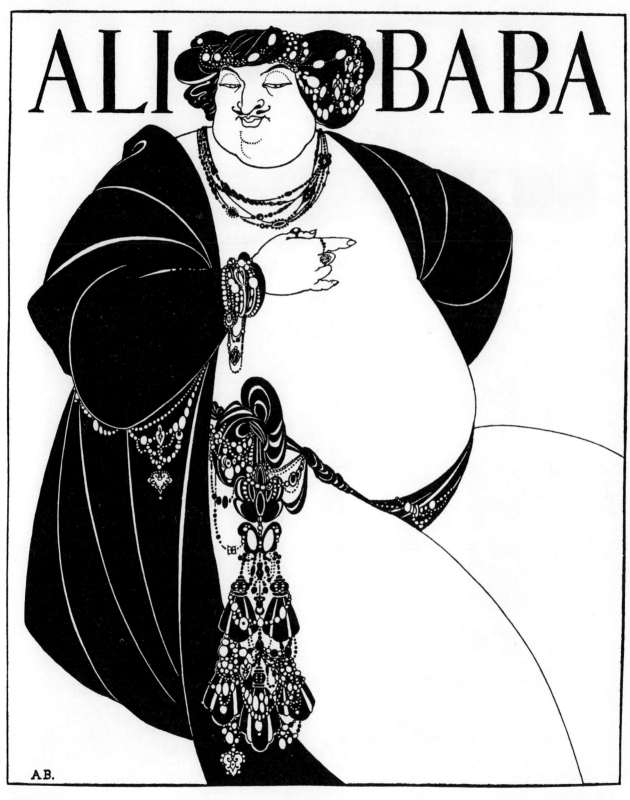

A.B.

Plate 155   COVER DESIGN FOR "THE FORTY THIEVES"

Plate 156

ALI BABA IN THE WOOD

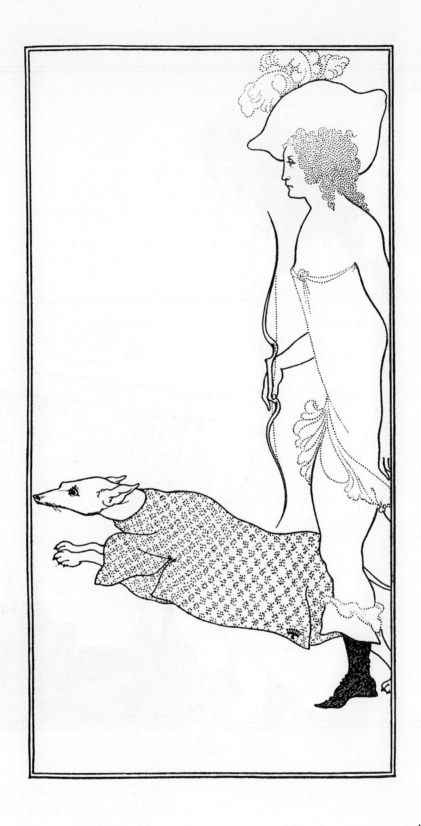

Plate 157   ATALANTA

MESSALINA.

Plate 158

MESSALINA RETURNING FROM
THE BATH ❧ ❧ ❧

Plate 159

COVER DESIGN. FROM
"THE HOUSES OF SIN"

Plate 160

LA DAME AUX CAMÉLIAS.
REPRODUCED BY PERMIS-
SION OF MR. R. B. ROSS

EX LIBRIS
OLIVE ·
CVSTANCE

A.B.

Plate 161

BOOK-PLATE.   BY   PERMISSION
OF MISS OLIVE CUSTANCE (LADY
ALFRED DOUGLAS) ❧ ❧ ❧

MADEMOISELLE DE MAUPIN

Aubrey Beardsley pinx

Plate 162

MADEMOISELLE DE MAUPIN
THIS DESIGN, WITH THE FIVE THAT
FOLLOW, APPEARED AS ILLUSTRATIONS
TO THÉOPHILE GAUTIER'S ROMANCE
"MADEMOISELLE DE MAUPIN"

Plate 163

D'ALBERT

Plate 164

D'ALBERT IN SEARCH
OF IDEALS ❧   ❧

Plate 165

THE LADY AT THE
DRESSING-TABLE

Plate 166   THE LADY WITH THE ROSE

Plate 167   THE LADY WITH THE MONKEY

Plate 168

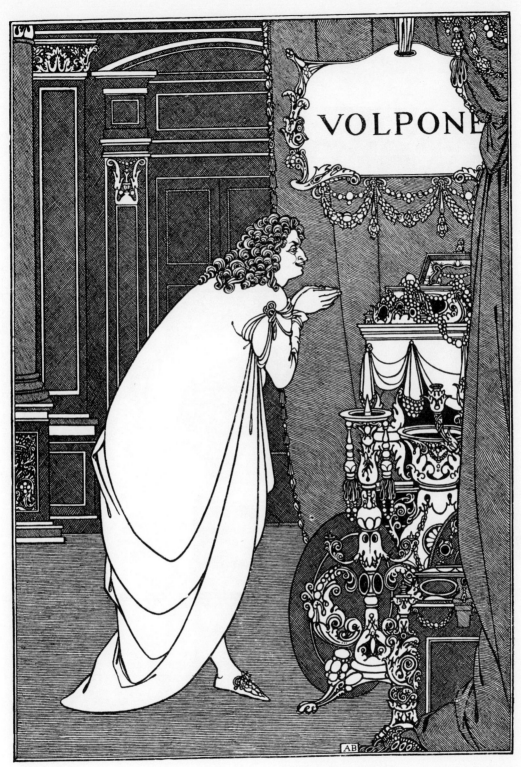

VOLPONE

Plate 169

FRONTISPIECE ☙ ☙ ☙
THIS AND THE FOLLOWING FIVE DESIGNS
ARE FROM "VOLPONE," BY BEN JONSON,
PUBLISHED BY JOHN LANE ☙ ☙

Plate 170

INITIAL

Plate 171

INITIAL

Plate 172

INITIAL

Plate 173

INITIAL

Plate 174

INITIAL

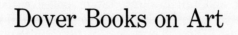
Dover Books on Art

MASTERPIECES OF FURNITURE, Verna Cook Salomonsky. Photographs and measured drawings of some of the finest examples of Colonial American, 17th century English, Windsor, Sheraton, Hepplewhite, Chippendale, Louis XIV, Queen Anne, and various other furniture styles. The textual matter includes information on traditions, characteristics, background, etc. of various pieces. 101 plates. Bibliography. 224pp. 7⅞ x 10¾.

21381-1 Paperbound $2.50

PRIMITIVE ART, Franz Boas. In this exhaustive volume, a great American anthropologist analyzes all the fundamental traits of primitive art, covering the formal element in art, representative art, symbolism, style, literature, music, and the dance. Illustrations of Indian embroidery, paleolithic paintings, woven blankets, wing and tail designs, totem poles, cutlery, earthenware, baskets and many other primitive objects and motifs. Over 900 illustrations. 376pp. 5⅜ x 8.   20025-6 Paperbound $2.50

AN INTRODUCTION TO A HISTORY OF WOODCUT, A. M. Hind. Nearly all of this authoritative 2-volume set is devoted to the 15th century—the period during which the woodcut came of age as an important art form. It is the most complete compendium of information on this period, the artists who contributed to it, and their technical and artistic accomplishments. Profusely illustrated with cuts by 15th century masters, and later works for comparative purposes. 484 illustrations. 5 indexes. Total of xi + 838pp. 5⅜ x 8½. Two-vols. 20952-0, 20953-0 Paperbound $5.50

A HISTORY OF ENGRAVING AND ETCHING, A. M. Hind. Beginning with the anonymous masters of 15th century engraving, this highly regarded and thorough survey carries you through Italy, Holland, and Germany to the great engravers and beginnings of etching in the 16th century, through the portrait engravers, master etchers, practicioners of mezzotint, crayon manner and stipple, aquatint, color prints, to modern etching in the period just prior to World War I. Beautifully illustrated —sharp clear prints on heavy opaque paper. Author's preface. 3 appendixes. 111 illustrations. xviii + 487 pp. 5⅜ x 8½.

20954-7 Paperbound $3.00

ART STUDENTS' ANATOMY, E. J. Farris. Teaching anatomy by using chiefly living objects for illustration, this study has enjoyed long popularity and success in art courses and home-study programs. All the basic elements of the human anatomy are illustrated in minute detail, diagrammed and pictured as they pass through common movements and actions. 158 drawings, photographs, and roentgenograms. Glossary of anatomical terms. x + 159pp. 5⅝ x 8⅜.   20744-7 Paperbound $1.50

COLONIAL LIGHTING, A. H. Hayward. The only book to cover the fascinating story of lamps and other lighting devices in America. Beginning with rush light holders used by the early settlers, it ranges through the elaborate chandeliers of the Federal period, illustrating 647 lamps. Of great value to antique collectors, designers, and historians of arts and crafts. Revised and enlarged by James R. Marsh. xxxi + 198pp. 5⅝ x 8¼.

20975-X Paperbound $2.00

Dover Books on Art

LANDSCAPE GARDENING IN JAPAN, Josiah Conder. A detailed picture of Japanese gardening techniques and ideas, the artistic principles incorporated in the Japanese garden, and the religious and ethical concepts at the heart of those principles. Preface. 92 illustrations, plus all 40 full-page plates from the Supplement. Index. xv + 299pp. 8⅜ x 11¼.

21216-5 Paperbound $3.50

DESIGN AND FIGURE CARVING, E. J. Tangerman. "Anyone who can peel a potato can carve," states the author, and in this unusual book he shows you how, covering every stage in detail from very simple exercises working up to museum-quality pieces. Terrific aid for hobbyists, arts and crafts counselors, teachers, those who wish to make reproductions for the commercial market. Appendix: How to Enlarge a Design. Brief bibliography. Index. 1298 figures. x + 289pp. 5⅜ x 8½.

21209-2 Paperbound $2.00

THE STANDARD BOOK OF QUILT MAKING AND COLLECTING, M. Ickis. Even if you are a beginner, you will soon find yourself quilting like an expert, by following these clearly drawn patterns, photographs, and step-by-step instructions. Learn how to plan the quilt, to select the pattern to harmonize with the design and color of the room, to choose materials. Over 40 full-size patterns. Index. 483 illustrations. One color plate. xi + 276pp. 6¾ x 9½.   20582-7 Paperbound $2.50

LOST EXAMPLES OF COLONIAL ARCHITECTURE, J. M. Howells. This book offers a unique guided tour through America's architectural past, all of which is either no longer in existence or so changed that its original beauty has been destroyed. More than 275 clear photos of old churches, dwelling houses, public buildings, business structures, etc. 245 plates, containing 281 photos and 9 drawings, floorplans, etc. New Index. xvii + 248pp. 7⅛ x 10¾.   21143-6 Paperbound $3.00

A HISTORY OF COSTUME, Carl Köhler. The most reliable and authentic account of the development of dress from ancient times through the 19th century. Based on actual pieces of clothing that have survived, using paintings, statues and other reproductions only where originals no longer exist. Hundreds of illustrations, including detailed patterns for many articles. Highly useful for theatre and movie directors, fashion designers, illustrators, teachers. Edited and augmented by Emma von Sichart. Translated by Alexander K. Dallas. 594 illustrations. 464pp. 5⅛ x 7⅛.

21030-8 Paperbound $3.00

Dover publishes books on commercial art, art history, crafts, design, art classics; also books on music, literature, science, mathematics, puzzles and entertainments, chess, engineering, biology, philosophy, psychology, languages, history, and other fields. For free circulars write to Dept. DA, Dover Publications, Inc., 180 Varick St., New York, N.Y. 10014.